Copyright © 2019 Nicole Creative Art
All right reserved.

IF FOUND PLEASE CONTACT:

NAME
....

ADDRESS
....

CITY   **STATE**   **ZIP**
....

E-MAIL
....

PHONE
....

CELL
....

PHOTO

SKETCH MAP OF TRAIL

FIRST VISIT ☐

RETURNING VISIT ☐

DATE: _____

TIME OF HIKE: _____

GPS COORDITIONS: _____

WEATHER CONDITIONS: _____

DISTANCE: _____

ELEVATION: _____

DIFFICULTY: _____

TRAIL TYPE: OUT& BACK   LOOP   ONE WAY
(CIRCLE ONE)   _____

DURATION OF HIKE: _____

PHOTOS/VIDEO IMAGES TAKEN: _____
(FILE NAME)

MAIN SIGHTS SEEN: _____

INTERESTING EVENTS NOTED: _____

FACILITIES/WATER AVAILABILITY: _____

PERSONS PRESENT: _____

GEAR, FOOD, BEVERAGE: _____

NOTES: PARKING, ENTRANCE _____

FEES, SHUTTLE, PETS, ROUTES _____

NOTES

IF FOUND PLEASE CONTACT:

NAME

....

ADDRESS

....

CITY   **STATE**   **ZIP**

....

E-MAIL

....

PHONE

....

CELL

....

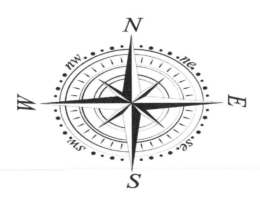

PHOTO

SKETCH MAP OF TRAIL

FIRST VISIT   ☐

RETURNING VISIT   ☐

DATE: _____

TIME OF HIKE: _____

GPS COORDITIONS: _____

WEATHER CONDITIONS: _____

DISTANCE: _____

ELEVATION: _____

DIFFICULTY: _____

TRAIL TYPE: OUT& BACK   LOOP   ONE WAY
(CIRCLE ONE)   _____

DURATION OF HIKE: _____

PHOTOS/VIDEO IMAGES TAKEN: _____
(FILE NAME)

MAIN SIGHTS SEEN: _____

INTERESTING EVENTS NOTED: _____

FACILITIES/WATER AVAILABILITY: _____

PERSONS PRESENT: _____

GEAR, FOOD, BEVERAGE: _____

NOTES: PARKING, ENTRANCE _____

FEES, SHUTTLE, PETS, ROUTES _____

NOTES

IF FOUND PLEASE CONTACT:

NAME

....

ADDRESS

....

CITY **STATE** **ZIP**

....

E-MAIL

....

PHONE

....

CELL

....

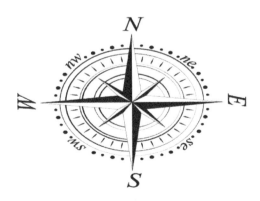

PHOTO

SKETCH MAP OF TRAIL

FIRST VISIT ☐

RETURNING VISIT ☐

DATE: _____

TIME OF HIKE: _____

GPS COORDITIONS: _____

WEATHER CONDITIONS: _____

DISTANCE: _____

ELEVATION: _____

DIFFICULTY: _____

TRAIL TYPE: OUT& BACK   LOOP   ONE WAY
(CIRCLE ONE)   _____

DURATION OF HIKE: _____

PHOTOS/VIDEO IMAGES TAKEN: _____
(FILE NAME)

MAIN SIGHTS SEEN: _____

INTERESTING EVENTS NOTED: _____

FACILITIES/WATER AVAILABILITY: _____

PERSONS PRESENT: _____

GEAR, FOOD, BEVERAGE: _____

NOTES: PARKING, ENTRANCE _____

FEES, SHUTTLE, PETS, ROUTES _____

NOTES

IF FOUND PLEASE CONTACT:

NAME

....

ADDRESS

....

CITY   **STATE**   **ZIP**

....

E-MAIL

....

PHONE

....

CELL

....

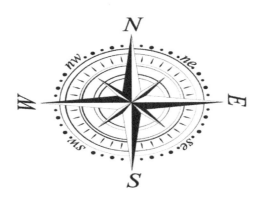

PHOTO

SKETCH MAP OF TRAIL

FIRST VISIT ☐

RETURNING VISIT ☐

DATE: _____

TIME OF HIKE: _____

GPS COORDITIONS: _____

WEATHER CONDITIONS: _____

DISTANCE: _____

ELEVATION: _____

DIFFICULTY: _____

TRAIL TYPE: OUT& BACK   LOOP   ONE WAY
(CIRCLE ONE)   _____

DURATION OF HIKE: _____

PHOTOS/VIDEO IMAGES TAKEN: _____
(FILE NAME)

MAIN SIGHTS SEEN: _____

INTERESTING EVENTS NOTED: _____

FACILITIES/WATER AVAILABILITY: _____

PERSONS PRESENT: _____

GEAR, FOOD, BEVERAGE: _____

NOTES: PARKING, ENTRANCE _____

FEES, SHUTTLE, PETS, ROUTES _____

NOTES

IF FOUND PLEASE CONTACT:

NAME

....

ADDRESS

....

CITY　　　　　　　　**STATE**　　　　**ZIP**

....

E-MAIL

....

PHONE

....

CELL

....

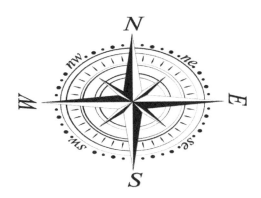

PHOTO

SKETCH MAP OF TRAIL

FIRST VISIT ☐

RETURNING VISIT ☐

DATE: _____

TIME OF HIKE: _____

GPS COORDITIONS: _____

WEATHER CONDITIONS: _____

DISTANCE: _____

ELEVATION: _____

DIFFICULTY: _____

TRAIL TYPE: OUT& BACK   LOOP   ONE WAY
(CIRCLE ONE)

DURATION OF HIKE: _____

PHOTOS/VIDEO IMAGES TAKEN: _____
(FILE NAME)

MAIN SIGHTS SEEN: _____

INTERESTING EVENTS NOTED: _____

FACILITIES/WATER AVAILABILITY: _____

PERSONS PRESENT: _____

GEAR, FOOD, BEVERAGE: _____

NOTES: PARKING, ENTRANCE FEES, SHUTTLE, PETS, ROUTES _____

NOTES

IF FOUND PLEASE CONTACT:

NAME

....

ADDRESS

....

CITY   **STATE**   **ZIP**

....

E-MAIL

....

PHONE

....

CELL

....

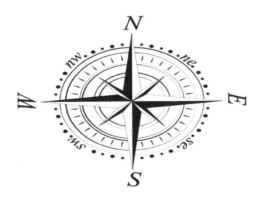

PHOTO

SKETCH MAP OF TRAIL

FIRST VISIT ☐

RETURNING VISIT ☐

DATE: _____

TIME OF HIKE: _____

GPS COORDITIONS: _____

WEATHER CONDITIONS: _____

DISTANCE: _____

ELEVATION: _____

DIFFICULTY: _____

TRAIL TYPE: OUT& BACK   LOOP   ONE WAY
(CIRCLE ONE) _____

DURATION OF HIKE: _____

PHOTOS/VIDEO IMAGES TAKEN: _____
(FILE NAME)

MAIN SIGHTS SEEN: _____

INTERESTING EVENTS NOTED: _____

FACILITIES/WATER AVAILABILITY: _____

PERSONS PRESENT: _____

GEAR, FOOD, BEVERAGE: _____

NOTES: PARKING, ENTRANCE _____

FEES, SHUTTLE, PETS, ROUTES _____

NOTES

IF FOUND PLEASE CONTACT:

NAME
....

ADDRESS
....

CITY   **STATE**   **ZIP**
....

E-MAIL
....

PHONE
....

CELL
....

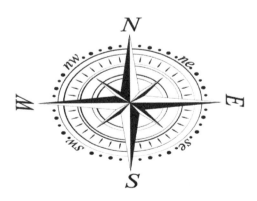

PHOTO

SKETCH MAP OF TRAIL

FIRST VISIT ☐

RETURNING VISIT ☐

DATE: _____

TIME OF HIKE: _____

GPS COORDITIONS: _____

WEATHER CONDITIONS: _____

DISTANCE: _____

ELEVATION: _____

DIFFICULTY: _____

TRAIL TYPE: OUT& BACK   LOOP   ONE WAY
(CIRCLE ONE)   _____

DURATION OF HIKE: _____

PHOTOS/VIDEO IMAGES TAKEN: _____
(FILE NAME)

MAIN SIGHTS SEEN: _____

INTERESTING EVENTS NOTED: _____

FACILITIES/WATER AVAILABILITY: _____

PERSONS PRESENT: _____

GEAR, FOOD, BEVERAGE: _____

NOTES: PARKING, ENTRANCE _____

FEES, SHUTTLE, PETS, ROUTES _____

NOTES

IF FOUND PLEASE CONTACT:

NAME

....

ADDRESS

....

CITY   **STATE**   **ZIP**

....

E-MAIL

....

PHONE

....

CELL

....

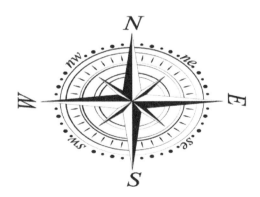

PHOTO

SKETCH MAP OF TRAIL

FIRST VISIT

RETURNING VISIT

DATE: _____

TIME OF HIKE: _____

GPS COORDITIONS: _____

WEATHER CONDITIONS: _____

DISTANCE: _____

ELEVATION: _____

DIFFICULTY: _____

TRAIL TYPE: OUT& BACK   LOOP   ONE WAY
(CIRCLE ONE) _____

DURATION OF HIKE: _____

PHOTOS/VIDEO IMAGES TAKEN: _____
(FILE NAME)

MAIN SIGHTS SEEN: _____

INTERESTING EVENTS NOTED: _____

FACILITIES/WATER AVAILABILITY: _____

PERSONS PRESENT: _____

GEAR, FOOD, BEVERAGE: _____

NOTES: PARKING, ENTRANCE _____

FEES, SHUTTLE, PETS, ROUTES _____

_____

NOTES

IF FOUND PLEASE CONTACT:

NAME

....

ADDRESS

....

CITY   **STATE**   **ZIP**

....

E-MAIL

....

PHONE

....

CELL

....

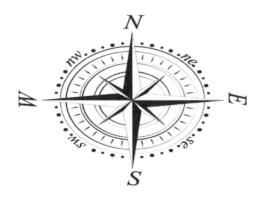

PHOTO

SKETCH MAP OF TRAIL

FIRST VISIT ☐

RETURNING VISIT ☐

DATE: _____

TIME OF HIKE: _____

GPS COORDITIONS: _____

WEATHER CONDITIONS: _____

DISTANCE: _____

ELEVATION: _____

DIFFICULTY: _____

TRAIL TYPE: OUT& BACK   LOOP   ONE WAY
(CIRCLE ONE)   _____

DURATION OF HIKE: _____

PHOTOS/VIDEO IMAGES TAKEN: _____
(FILE NAME)

MAIN SIGHTS SEEN: _____

INTERESTING EVENTS NOTED: _____

FACILITIES/WATER AVAILABILITY: _____

PERSONS PRESENT: _____

GEAR, FOOD, BEVERAGE: _____

NOTES: PARKING, ENTRANCE _____

FEES, SHUTTLE, PETS, ROUTES _____

NOTES

IF FOUND PLEASE CONTACT:

NAME

....

ADDRESS

....

CITY   **STATE**   **ZIP**

....

E-MAIL

....

PHONE

....

CELL

....

PHOTO

SKETCH MAP OF TRAIL

FIRST VISIT ☐

RETURNING VISIT ☐

DATE: _____

TIME OF HIKE: _____

GPS COORDITIONS: _____

WEATHER CONDITIONS: _____

DISTANCE: _____

ELEVATION: _____

DIFFICULTY: _____

TRAIL TYPE: OUT& BACK   LOOP   ONE WAY
(CIRCLE ONE)   _____

DURATION OF HIKE: _____

PHOTOS/VIDEO IMAGES TAKEN: _____
(FILE NAME)

MAIN SIGHTS SEEN: _____

INTERESTING EVENTS NOTED: _____

FACILITIES/WATER AVAILABILITY: _____

PERSONS PRESENT: _____

GEAR, FOOD, BEVERAGE: _____

NOTES: PARKING, ENTRANCE   _____

FEES, SHUTTLE, PETS, ROUTES _____

NOTES

IF FOUND PLEASE CONTACT:

NAME
....

ADDRESS
....

CITY   **STATE**   **ZIP**
....

E-MAIL
....

PHONE
....

CELL
....

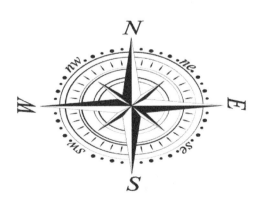

PHOTO

SKETCH MAP OF TRAIL

FIRST VISIT ☐

RETURNING VISIT ☐

DATE: _____

TIME OF HIKE: _____

GPS COORDITIONS: _____

WEATHER CONDITIONS: _____

DISTANCE: _____

ELEVATION: _____

DIFFICULTY: _____

TRAIL TYPE: OUT& BACK   LOOP   ONE WAY
(CIRCLE ONE) _____

DURATION OF HIKE: _____

PHOTOS/VIDEO IMAGES TAKEN: _____
(FILE NAME)

MAIN SIGHTS SEEN: _____

INTERESTING EVENTS NOTED: _____

FACILITIES/WATER AVAILABILITY: _____

PERSONS PRESENT: _____

GEAR, FOOD, BEVERAGE: _____

NOTES: PARKING, ENTRANCE _____
FEES, SHUTTLE, PETS, ROUTES _____

NOTES

IF FOUND PLEASE CONTACT:

NAME

....

ADDRESS

....

CITY   **STATE**   **ZIP**

....

E-MAIL

....

PHONE

....

CELL

....

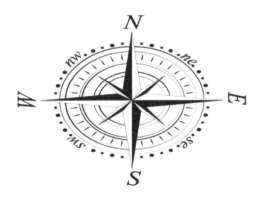

PHOTO

SKETCH MAP OF TRAIL

FIRST VISIT

RETURNING VISIT

DATE: _____

TIME OF HIKE: _____

GPS COORDITIONS: _____

WEATHER CONDITIONS: _____

DISTANCE: _____

ELEVATION: _____

DIFFICULTY: _____

TRAIL TYPE: OUT& BACK   LOOP   ONE WAY
(CIRCLE ONE)   _____

DURATION OF HIKE: _____

PHOTOS/VIDEO IMAGES TAKEN: _____
(FILE NAME)

MAIN SIGHTS SEEN: _____

INTERESTING EVENTS NOTED: _____

FACILITIES/WATER AVAILABILITY: _____

PERSONS PRESENT: _____

GEAR, FOOD, BEVERAGE: _____

NOTES: PARKING, ENTRANCE _____

FEES, SHUTTLE, PETS, ROUTES _____

NOTES

IF FOUND PLEASE CONTACT:

NAME

....

ADDRESS

....

CITY   **STATE**   **ZIP**

....

E-MAIL

....

PHONE

....

CELL

....

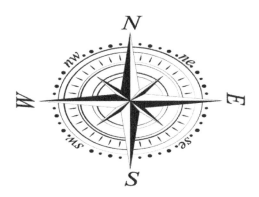

PHOTO

SKETCH MAP OF TRAIL

FIRST VISIT

RETURNING VISIT

DATE: _____

TIME OF HIKE: _____

GPS COORDITIONS: _____

WEATHER CONDITIONS: _____

DISTANCE: _____

ELEVATION: _____

DIFFICULTY: _____

TRAIL TYPE: OUT& BACK   LOOP   ONE WAY
(CIRCLE ONE)   _____

DURATION OF HIKE: _____

PHOTOS/VIDEO IMAGES TAKEN: _____
(FILE NAME)

MAIN SIGHTS SEEN: _____

INTERESTING EVENTS NOTED: _____

FACILITIES/WATER AVAILABILITY: _____

PERSONS PRESENT: _____

GEAR, FOOD, BEVERAGE: _____

NOTES: PARKING, ENTRANCE _____

FEES, SHUTTLE, PETS, ROUTES _____

_____

NOTES

IF FOUND PLEASE CONTACT:

NAME

....

ADDRESS

....

CITY   **STATE**   **ZIP**

....

E-MAIL

....

PHONE

....

CELL

....

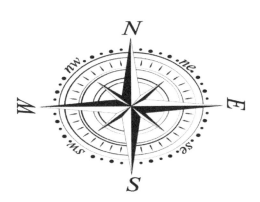

PHOTO

SKETCH MAP OF TRAIL

FIRST VISIT ☐

RETURNING VISIT ☐

DATE: _____

TIME OF HIKE: _____

GPS COORDITIONS: _____

WEATHER CONDITIONS: _____

DISTANCE: _____

ELEVATION: _____

DIFFICULTY: _____

TRAIL TYPE: OUT& BACK   LOOP   ONE WAY
(CIRCLE ONE)   _____

DURATION OF HIKE: _____

PHOTOS/VIDEO IMAGES TAKEN: _____
(FILE NAME)

MAIN SIGHTS SEEN: _____

INTERESTING EVENTS NOTED: _____

FACILITIES/WATER AVAILABILITY: _____

PERSONS PRESENT: _____

GEAR, FOOD, BEVERAGE: _____

NOTES: PARKING, ENTRANCE _____

FEES, SHUTTLE, PETS, ROUTES _____

NOTES

IF FOUND PLEASE CONTACT:

NAME
....

ADDRESS
....

CITY   **STATE**   **ZIP**
....

E-MAIL
....

PHONE
....

CELL
....

PHOTO

SKETCH MAP OF TRAIL

FIRST VISIT ☐
RETURNING VISIT ☐

DATE: _____

TIME OF HIKE: _____

GPS COORDITIONS: _____

WEATHER CONDITIONS: _____

DISTANCE: _____

ELEVATION: _____

DIFFICULTY: _____

TRAIL TYPE: OUT& BACK   LOOP   ONE WAY
(CIRCLE ONE)

DURATION OF HIKE: _____

PHOTOS/VIDEO IMAGES TAKEN: _____
(FILE NAME)

MAIN SIGHTS SEEN: _____

INTERESTING EVENTS NOTED: _____

FACILITIES/WATER AVAILABILITY: _____

PERSONS PRESENT: _____

GEAR, FOOD, BEVERAGE: _____

NOTES: PARKING, ENTRANCE

FEES, SHUTTLE, PETS, ROUTES _____

NOTES

IF FOUND PLEASE CONTACT:

NAME
....

ADDRESS
....

CITY   **STATE**   **ZIP**
....

E-MAIL
....

PHONE
....

CELL
....

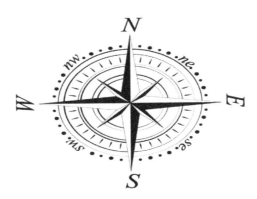

PHOTO

SKETCH MAP OF TRAIL

FIRST VISIT ☐

RETURNING VISIT ☐

DATE: _____

TIME OF HIKE: _____

GPS COORDITIONS: _____

WEATHER CONDITIONS: _____

DISTANCE: _____

ELEVATION: _____

DIFFICULTY: _____

TRAIL TYPE: OUT& BACK   LOOP   ONE WAY
(CIRCLE ONE)   _____

DURATION OF HIKE: _____

PHOTOS/VIDEO IMAGES TAKEN: _____
(FILE NAME)

MAIN SIGHTS SEEN: _____

INTERESTING EVENTS NOTED: _____

FACILITIES/WATER AVAILABILITY: _____

PERSONS PRESENT: _____

GEAR, FOOD, BEVERAGE: _____

NOTES: PARKING, ENTRANCE _____

FEES, SHUTTLE, PETS, ROUTES _____

NOTES

IF FOUND PLEASE CONTACT:

NAME

....

ADDRESS

....

CITY   **STATE**   **ZIP**

....

E-MAIL

....

PHONE

....

CELL

....

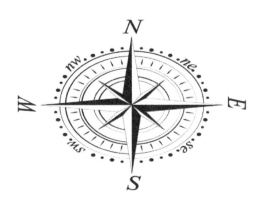

PHOTO

SKETCH MAP OF TRAIL

FIRST VISIT ☐

RETURNING VISIT ☐

DATE: _____

TIME OF HIKE: _____

GPS COORDITIONS: _____

WEATHER CONDITIONS: _____

DISTANCE: _____

ELEVATION: _____

DIFFICULTY: _____

TRAIL TYPE: OUT& BACK   LOOP   ONE WAY
(CIRCLE ONE) _____

DURATION OF HIKE: _____

PHOTOS/VIDEO IMAGES TAKEN: _____
(FILE NAME)

MAIN SIGHTS SEEN: _____

INTERESTING EVENTS NOTED: _____

FACILITIES/WATER AVAILABILITY: _____

PERSONS PRESENT: _____

GEAR, FOOD, BEVERAGE: _____

NOTES: PARKING, ENTRANCE FEES, SHUTTLE, PETS, ROUTES _____

NOTES

IF FOUND PLEASE CONTACT:

NAME

....

ADDRESS

....

CITY   **STATE**   **ZIP**

....

E-MAIL

....

PHONE

....

CELL

....

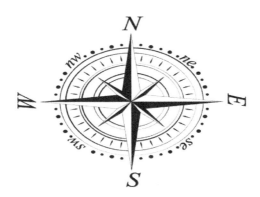

PHOTO

SKETCH MAP OF TRAIL

FIRST VISIT ☐

RETURNING VISIT ☐

DATE: _____

TIME OF HIKE: _____

GPS COORDITIONS: _____

WEATHER CONDITIONS: _____

DISTANCE: _____

ELEVATION: _____

DIFFICULTY: _____

TRAIL TYPE: OUT& BACK   LOOP   ONE WAY
(CIRCLE ONE)   _____

DURATION OF HIKE: _____

PHOTOS/VIDEO IMAGES TAKEN: _____
(FILE NAME)

MAIN SIGHTS SEEN: _____

INTERESTING EVENTS NOTED: _____

FACILITIES/WATER AVAILABILITY: _____

PERSONS PRESENT: _____

GEAR, FOOD, BEVERAGE: _____

NOTES: PARKING, ENTRANCE _____

FEES, SHUTTLE, PETS, ROUTES _____

NOTES

IF FOUND PLEASE CONTACT:

NAME

....

ADDRESS

....

CITY   **STATE**   **ZIP**

....

E-MAIL

....

PHONE

....

CELL

....

PHOTO

SKETCH MAP OF TRAIL

FIRST VISIT

RETURNING VISIT

DATE: _____

TIME OF HIKE: _____

GPS COORDITIONS: _____

WEATHER CONDITIONS: _____

DISTANCE: _____

ELEVATION: _____

DIFFICULTY: _____

TRAIL TYPE: OUT& BACK   LOOP   ONE WAY
(CIRCLE ONE)   _____

DURATION OF HIKE: _____

PHOTOS/VIDEO IMAGES TAKEN: _____
(FILE NAME)

MAIN SIGHTS SEEN: _____

INTERESTING EVENTS NOTED: _____

FACILITIES/WATER AVAILABILITY: _____

PERSONS PRESENT: _____

GEAR, FOOD, BEVERAGE: _____

NOTES: PARKING, ENTRANCE _____

FEES, SHUTTLE, PETS, ROUTES _____

NOTES

IF FOUND PLEASE CONTACT:

NAME
....

ADDRESS
....

CITY　　　　　　　　**STATE**　　　　**ZIP**
....

E-MAIL
....

PHONE
....

CELL
....

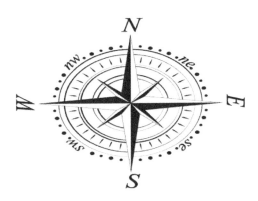

PHOTO

SKETCH MAP OF TRAIL

FIRST VISIT ☐

RETURNING VISIT ☐

DATE: _____

TIME OF HIKE: _____

GPS COORDITIONS: _____

WEATHER CONDITIONS: _____

DISTANCE: _____

ELEVATION: _____

DIFFICULTY: _____

TRAIL TYPE: OUT& BACK   LOOP   ONE WAY
(CIRCLE ONE)   _____

DURATION OF HIKE: _____

PHOTOS/VIDEO IMAGES TAKEN: _____
(FILE NAME)

MAIN SIGHTS SEEN: _____

INTERESTING EVENTS NOTED: _____

FACILITIES/WATER AVAILABILITY: _____

PERSONS PRESENT: _____

GEAR, FOOD, BEVERAGE: _____

NOTES: PARKING, ENTRANCE FEES, SHUTTLE, PETS, ROUTES _____

NOTES

IF FOUND PLEASE CONTACT:

NAME

....

ADDRESS

....

CITY **STATE** **ZIP**

....

E-MAIL

....

PHONE

....

CELL

....

PHOTO

SKETCH MAP OF TRAIL

FIRST VISIT

RETURNING VISIT

DATE: _____

TIME OF HIKE: _____

GPS COORDITIONS: _____

WEATHER CONDITIONS: _____

DISTANCE: _____

ELEVATION: _____

DIFFICULTY: _____

TRAIL TYPE: OUT& BACK   LOOP   ONE WAY
(CIRCLE ONE)   _____

DURATION OF HIKE: _____

PHOTOS/VIDEO IMAGES TAKEN: _____
(FILE NAME)

MAIN SIGHTS SEEN: _____

INTERESTING EVENTS NOTED: _____

FACILITIES/WATER AVAILABILITY: _____

PERSONS PRESENT: _____

GEAR, FOOD, BEVERAGE: _____

NOTES: PARKING, ENTRANCE _____

FEES, SHUTTLE, PETS, ROUTES _____

NOTES

IF FOUND PLEASE CONTACT:

NAME
....

ADDRESS
....

CITY   **STATE**   **ZIP**
....

E-MAIL
....

PHONE
....

CELL
....

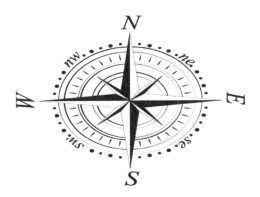

PHOTO

SKETCH MAP OF TRAIL

FIRST VISIT ☐

RETURNING VISIT ☐

DATE: _____

TIME OF HIKE: _____

GPS COORDITIONS: _____

WEATHER CONDITIONS: _____

DISTANCE: _____

ELEVATION: _____

DIFFICULTY: _____

TRAIL TYPE: OUT& BACK   LOOP   ONE WAY
(CIRCLE ONE)   _____

DURATION OF HIKE: _____

PHOTOS/VIDEO IMAGES TAKEN: _____
(FILE NAME)

MAIN SIGHTS SEEN: _____

INTERESTING EVENTS NOTED: _____

FACILITIES/WATER AVAILABILITY: _____

PERSONS PRESENT: _____

GEAR, FOOD, BEVERAGE: _____

NOTES: PARKING, ENTRANCE _____

FEES, SHUTTLE, PETS, ROUTES _____

_____

NOTES

IF FOUND PLEASE CONTACT:

NAME
....

ADDRESS
....

CITY   **STATE**   **ZIP**
....

E-MAIL
....

PHONE
....

CELL
....

PHOTO

SKETCH MAP OF TRAIL

FIRST VISIT

RETURNING VISIT

DATE: _____

TIME OF HIKE: _____

GPS COORDITIONS: _____

WEATHER CONDITIONS: _____

DISTANCE: _____

ELEVATION: _____

DIFFICULTY: _____

TRAIL TYPE: OUT& BACK   LOOP   ONE WAY
(CIRCLE ONE)   _____

DURATION OF HIKE: _____

PHOTOS/VIDEO IMAGES TAKEN: _____
(FILE NAME)

MAIN SIGHTS SEEN: _____

INTERESTING EVENTS NOTED: _____

FACILITIES/WATER AVAILABILITY: _____

PERSONS PRESENT: _____

GEAR, FOOD, BEVERAGE: _____

NOTES: PARKING, ENTRANCE _____

FEES, SHUTTLE, PETS, ROUTES _____

NOTES

IF FOUND PLEASE CONTACT:

NAME

....

ADDRESS

....

CITY   **STATE**   **ZIP**

....

E-MAIL

....

PHONE

....

CELL

....

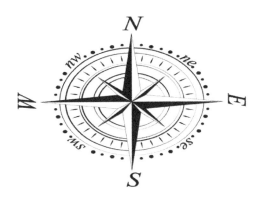

PHOTO

SKETCH MAP OF TRAIL

FIRST VISIT ☐

RETURNING VISIT ☐

DATE: _____

TIME OF HIKE: _____

GPS COORDITIONS: _____

WEATHER CONDITIONS: _____

DISTANCE: _____

ELEVATION: _____

DIFFICULTY: _____

TRAIL TYPE: OUT& BACK   LOOP   ONE WAY
(CIRCLE ONE) _____

DURATION OF HIKE: _____

PHOTOS/VIDEO IMAGES TAKEN: _____
(FILE NAME)

MAIN SIGHTS SEEN: _____

INTERESTING EVENTS NOTED: _____

FACILITIES/WATER AVAILABILITY: _____

PERSONS PRESENT: _____

GEAR, FOOD, BEVERAGE: _____

NOTES: PARKING, ENTRANCE _____

FEES, SHUTTLE, PETS, ROUTES _____

NOTES

IF FOUND PLEASE CONTACT:

NAME

....

ADDRESS

....

CITY   **STATE**   **ZIP**

....

E-MAIL

....

PHONE

....

CELL

....

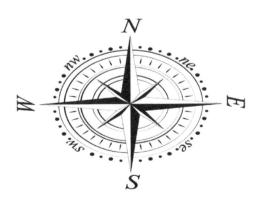

PHOTO

SKETCH MAP OF TRAIL

FIRST VISIT ☐

RETURNING VISIT ☐

DATE: _____

TIME OF HIKE: _____

GPS COORDITIONS: _____

WEATHER CONDITIONS: _____

DISTANCE: _____

ELEVATION: _____

DIFFICULTY: _____

TRAIL TYPE: OUT& BACK   LOOP   ONE WAY
(CIRCLE ONE) _____

DURATION OF HIKE: _____

PHOTOS/VIDEO IMAGES TAKEN: _____
(FILE NAME)

MAIN SIGHTS SEEN: _____

INTERESTING EVENTS NOTED: _____

FACILITIES/WATER AVAILABILITY: _____

PERSONS PRESENT: _____

GEAR, FOOD, BEVERAGE: _____

NOTES: PARKING, ENTRANCE _____

FEES, SHUTTLE, PETS, ROUTES _____

NOTES

NOTES

NOTES

NOTES

NOTES

NOTES

NOTES

NOTES

NOTES

NOTES

NOTES

NOTES

NOTES

NOTES

NOTES

NOTES

NOTES

NOTES

NOTES

Made in the USA
Middletown, DE
15 April 2025

74354226R00070